IMAGES
of America

AROUND BENNINGTON

On the Cover: A house is pictured being moved up Allen Street in Bennington around 1915. (Courtesy of the Bennington Historical Society.)

IMAGES
of America

AROUND BENNINGTON

Gordon A. Mueller
Foreword by Jeffrey S. Spencer

ARCADIA
PUBLISHING

ISBN 978-1-4671-0624-5

Published by Arcadia Publishing
Charleston, South Carolina

Printed in the United States of America

Library of Congress Control Number: 2020947745

For all general information, please contact Arcadia Publishing:
Telephone 843-853-2070
Fax 843-853-0044
E-mail sales@arcadiapublishing.com
For customer service and orders:
Toll-Free 1-888-313-2665

Visit us on the Internet at www.arcadiapublishing.com

*This book is dedicated to Linda: my wife,
my best friend, and my partner.*

Contents

ACKNOWLEDGMENTS

It is said a picture is worth a thousand words. The images in this book tell the story of how the people around Bennington made a living—their loves, their dreams, their hardships, and their successes. They span 75 years, from 1889 to 1964, and they reveal what it was like growing up in a small railroad town in eastern Nebraska.

Unless otherwise noted, all images appear courtesy of the Bennington Historical Society. This collection includes images previously shared by the City of Bennington and from local family collections. In particular, I thank Weyland Magee for sharing his family's amazing collection, and Bennington Historical Society members and others who shared their photographs and memories.

Four previous works provided material for this project. St. John's Lutheran Church published "Golden Jubilee" in 1948 and "Centennial Report" in 1998, describing the church's history. Helen Braesch, Ila Mohr, and the Bennington Woman's Club wrote a broader historical account of the community in *1967: Nebraska's Centennial Year and Bennington's 80th Year.* Edna Mohr and Gary Sather edited the Bennington Centennial Book Committee's *Bennington, Nebraska: 1892–1992*, which included a great deal of historical information on the community, its businesses, and family histories. Some of their images were used in this project.

Very special thanks go to a dear friend and mentor, Jeffery Spencer, without whose encouragement and guidance this project would never have happened. His love and dedication to the preservation of local history is contagious.

The author's proceeds from the sale of this book will go to support Bennington Historical Society projects.

FOREWORD

The advent of the railroad in the second half of the 19th century ushered in unparalleled growth and development throughout the United States. Nowhere was this more evident than in the Midwest, including the state of Nebraska. After the large urban area of Omaha was settled in what became Douglas County in the 1850s, various railroad companies branched out into the adjacent undeveloped countryside. The town of Bennington was one of the new communities to take advantage of the rail lines.

By the turn of the 20th century, Bennington was a thriving community. As the vast majority of the surrounding area was rural and agricultural, it served as an important commercial and cultural hub for the local population. It soon became the center of community life, with shops, businesses, and service providers, as well as places of entertainment and recreation.

In today's world of rapid transportation and instantaneous communication, it is difficult to visualize how life would have been in this small, rural town. Certainly we can understand that a picture is worth a thousand words, and so each of the photographs reproduced in this book has its own story to tell.

Gordon Mueller is a fourth-generation direct descendant of some of the original settlers in the community. Long interested in local history, he has assembled here a collection of unique photographic images that provide us with a detailed picture of this pioneer town. Each image is accompanied by a descriptive caption that in itself provides much informative history.

We commend Arcadia Publishing for its vision in the development and production of its Images of America series. This important series has gathered, preserved, and made available to a general readership vast quantities of local history, much of which otherwise would have been lost. As well, we are very pleased that the photographic story of Bennington, Nebraska, could be included in this story. That history, as shown through these images, pays tribute to all those who were a part of the endeavor that brought the community into being and moved it forward. It is this story, replicated countless times, which has been so significant in the building of our great country.

It is our hope that the images and descriptions included here will inform and instruct as well as kindle many fond and pleasant memories connecting us to this place and its unique and interesting history.

—Jeffrey S. Spencer

Introduction

Bennington sits at the crossroads of our country's exploration and westward migration. The Missouri and Platte Rivers were important travel corridors for American Indians, European explorers, trappers, and pioneers. Several important historical events happened within a 15-mile radius of Bennington.

Physical evidence of the indigenous tribes has faded over time, but their presence has been immortalized through the use of their names. Nebraska is derived from the Otoe word *Nebrathka*, meaning "flat water," a reference to the Platte River. Many Nebraska towns take their names from Indian tribes: Omaha, Pawnee City, Nemaha, Tekamah, Tecumseh, Oto, Ogallala, Brule, Arapahoe, Ponca, Red Cloud, and Winnebago, to name a few.

A landmark civil rights ruling occurred a century and a half ago just 10 miles east of Bennington. Chief Standing Bear of the Ponca tribe stood before a federal judge at Fort Omaha and said the famous words "God made me, therefore I am human." The judge agreed with the chief, acknowledging that Indians were humans and had civil rights. The precedent was established, but the struggle continued. Standing Bear Reservoir just south of town is named in his honor, and recently Sen. Ben Sass placed a statue in the state capitol rotunda to honor the chief's memory.

The French flag once flew over this part of the country until the United States bought the Louisiana Purchase from Napoleon Bonaparte. In 1804, Pres. Thomas Jefferson sent Meriwether Lewis and William Clark to explore these lands, and their expedition traveled up the Missouri River just 12 miles east of Bennington. They camped a few days near the current town of Fort Calhoun, where they met with local Indian tribes at Council Bluffs.

Other travelers soon followed. Manuel Lisa came up the river in 1806 and established a trading post named Fort Lisa for the Missouri Fur Company. The trading post was at the current site of North Dodge Park in Omaha.

When Lewis and Clark reported back to the government, they recommended that Congress appropriate funds to build a fort at Council Bluffs, and Congress did. The US Army established Fort Atkinson in 1819, and it became the largest Army post west of the Missouri River. It was so isolated that one winter when the garrison could not be resupplied, nearly half its men died of starvation and scurvy.

The US Department of War started an unusual experiment to see if soldiers could also be part-time farmers and produce their own food. Not only did they produce enough for their own needs, they had surpluses, which they sold. However, critics complained that this was a distraction from soldiering. The experiment was soon dropped, but not before it illustrated the agricultural potential of this land.

Lt. Stephen Long arrived at Fort Lisa during the spring of 1819 on the first steam-powered river boat to navigate this far upstream. His orders were to map the Missouri, Platte, and Elkhorn River drainages. He described the Great Plains as "the Great American Desert."

Despite Long's description, interest in opening up the Great Plains grew. John Fremont explored the Platte River and described and mapped the Oregon Trail in 1842. The "Pathfinder's" descriptions and road map to the West was an instant hit with the public. His maps were so popular that they were published by the US Senate in 1846 and became the common map used by pioneers traveling west. That same year, Iowa achieved statehood.

Members of the Church of Jesus Christ of Latter-day Saints, or Mormons, were being persecuted. Their leader, Joseph Smith, had been jailed and later murdered by an angry mob in Nauvoo, Illinois. Church members were physically forced to leave their homes. Church elders led members to western Iowa, where nearly 3,000 gathered along the eastern shore of the Missouri River. The area west of the Missouri River was frontier, or Indian territory, and pioneers were not allowed to settle there. However, to avoid further conflict, church leaders proposed to build a temporary compound on the west side of the river in 1846. The Omaha tribe and Indian agent consented on the condition that the settlement be vacated within two years. The Mormons built more than 700 temporary structures and named the encampment the Winter Quarters. That winter was brutally cold, and nearly 700 perished from malnutrition and disease. Their push to Utah continued the following spring, and the Nebraska settlement was abandoned as promised.

The Mormons established a trail within sight of Bennington that was traveled by an estimated 70,000 pioneers heading west between 1846 and 1865. Peak use was in the early 1850s, as hundreds of wagons lined up on the eastern shore of the Missouri River waiting their turn to cross by ferryboat. Pioneers were heading west to start new lives—some to avoid religious persecution, some as farmers and ranchers, others as business owners, and some to find their riches in the goldfields. The rich and fertile lands they passed through made an impression.

Congress passed the Kansas-Nebraska Act in 1854, creating the Kansas and Nebraska Territories and thus allowing settlement west of the Missouri River. Prior to this time, there were only temporary settlements such as the Mormon Winter Quarters, trading posts like Fort Lisa, and military posts like Fort Atkinson. However, Belleview had been an active trading settlement at the mouth of the Platte River since the 1830s, helping to justify its claim of being Nebraska's oldest town. Omaha and Florence were founded in 1854 and Fort Calhoun in 1855.

Pres. Abraham Lincoln signed the Pacific Railroad Act in 1862, which charged the Central Pacific and Union Pacific Railroads to build a transcontinental rail line from Omaha to the West Coast. Work began in 1863, and the project ended at Promontory Point, Utah, in 1869.

Towns along the rail lines grew. Some were successful, but many were poorly conceived and failed to survive. Competition intensified as railroads expanded through the countryside. The Fremont, Elkhorn & Missouri Valley Railroad formed the Pioneer Townsite Company in 1886. It integrated town planning with new rail line construction. Initially, this arrangement benefitted both the railroad and the communities it started. They were mutually dependent upon each other. However, community dependence on rail service began to erode with the arrival of the horseless carriage. By 1975, the rail line that created Bennington and Washington had been abandoned and removed. Bennington continued to grow due to its proximity to Omaha, while Washington's business community declined, and it eventually closed its school and church.

One

Some Early Settlers

The passage of the Kansas-Nebraska Act in 1854 set the stage for the settlement of the Midwest. Early entrepreneurs set up businesses along the Mormon Trail to assist pioneers traveling west. A ferry was built on the Elkhorn River where pioneers could cross. One of the first inland outposts was Elkhorn City, on the bluff east of the ferry crossing. Pioneer diaries suggest that Elkhorn City was the last place travelers were able to buy fresh milk and cheese before continuing into the Platte Valley.

A few years later, Elkhorn City had a store, stagecoach stop, and post office. Farther down the trail, early entrepreneurs sold travelers supplies and prairie hay, which had become scarce due to overgrazing along the trail. The Indian raid on the Martin brothers near Alda, Nebraska, illustrates the opportunities and risks for these early settlers.

The government surveyed an east-to-west road across Nebraska in 1857 that generally followed the Mormon and Oregon Trails. It connected Fort Omaha with the western military bases and was appropriately named Military Road.

The federal government deeded a great deal of land to the railroads, which they in turn sold to help finance the transcontinental railroad project. Land was also given to veterans and other citizens in lieu of money for their service. The land under Bennington, for example, was given to Joseph Tuttle as payment for his military service during the War of 1812. The passage of the Homestead Act in 1862 allowed anyone to file for 160 acres of free land. A great many European immigrants came to take advantage of it. In this area, many came from Schleswig-Holstein, in what is now northern Germany. That area of Europe had experienced unrest and war through much of the 1800s.

The government established frontier post offices in the late 1870s; the two closest were Blakely and Hayes. Blakely was on the Military Road just four miles southwest of the current site of Bennington. Hayes was on a freight road two miles north. Both had a few small buildings, possibly a smithy to make minor repairs, a small store, and a residence for the operators. Mail was delivered by horse or stagecoach to these outposts, and they became important connections to the outside world for early settlers. This is where early letters were mailed encouraging other family members, cousins, and friends to immigrate to America. The result suggests that many letters were written in German.

Charles Frederic Gottsch was the son of Claus Gottsch, one of the earliest pioneers to settle in the Bennington area. Claus Gottsch emigrated from Schleswig-Holstein and initially settled near Davenport, Iowa, in 1853. His family bought land and moved near Washington County in 1858. Claus died in 1878, but his son Charles took over the homestead. Charles married, and the couple had children of their own. A son, Otto, lived on the Gottsch homestead until he was 99 years old. The farm continues to be owned by the Gottsch family.

Henry Schneider and his twin brother, Hans, were born in 1834. Their father was killed by poachers in Germany, and their mother married Claus Gottsch, who settled here in 1858. The brothers homesteaded in Washington County. They purchased land from Claus Oft and built the first saloon in Bennington. (Courtesy of the Washington County Museum.)

Hans Schneider homesteaded near his brother's farm in Washington County. The brothers opened the first saloon in Bennington in 1887; it was located west of 156th Street near the railroad tracks. Hans became town marshal in Bennington and later went on to become Washington County sheriff. (Courtesy of the Washington County Museum.)

Hans and Anna Schneekloth are pictured here. Hans emigrated from Schleswig-Holstein and served with the US Cavalry during the Civil War guarding wagon trains and supply shipments traveling between Fort Kearny and Fort Laramie. He married and settled on a farm east of Bennington after leaving the Army. The couple had a daughter, but Anna died when the child was only six years old. Hans later married Anna Kuhl.

Gustave "Gus" Bunz was the son of Peter Bunz II, who sold a portion of his farm to the Pioneer Townsite Company to create Bennington. Local residents at the time wanted the new town name to be "Bunztown." Gus was born in 1876 on the family home place just east of Bennington. He married Katherine Timme and started a farm equipment business with his brother in law Charles Timme. Bunz served on Bennington's village board for several years.

Claus Oft married Antje Kramer, a widow, in 1878. He served on the first school board and was a charter member of St. John's Lutheran Church. He built and operated a gristmill on the Papio Creek and was active in politics. At a rally, Oft suffered a broken leg in an altercation. He sued for damages, and the case went to the Nebraska Supreme Court, where he won.

Eggert Oft came to America with his family in 1869 and later moved to the Bennington area with his brother Claus. Eggert bought a farm just west of the proposed town in 1879. He married Rosa Lage in 1882, and they had five children. Eggert bought nine lots and built a hotel, saloon, livery stable, and blacksmith shop. He served on the first village board and was a charter member of St. John's Lutheran Church.

Gustav Paulsen is pictured with his son Fredrick. Gustav came to the Bennington area to farm in 1875. However, with the creation of Washington, he purchased a lot and started a blacksmith shop there. Seeing that Bennington was growing faster, he physically moved his business and home to Bennington two years later. He operated a saloon and served on the village board. He and his wife had eight children.

Fred and Lenna Gottsch emigrated from Schleswig-Holstein in the 1870s. The couple purchased a farm at 156th and Ida Streets in 1876 and started a proud family legacy of farmers and business professionals in the Bennington community.

George Ohrt emigrated in the 1860s from Schleswig-Holstein, where he had been a schoolteacher. He settled just across the Washington County line, where he farmed for 35 years until his death in 1910. He had two sons, George and Fred, who took over the family farm.

Peter and Augusta Backhuus celebrate their 50th wedding anniversary in 1935. The couple emigrated from Schleswig-Holstein, where Peter had been a carpenter. They married in 1885 and settled on a farm on 156th Street and Military Road. They had seven children: Minnie, Peter II, Iva Pearl, Frank, Maggie, Etta, and Elmer. (Courtesy of Nancy Mohr.)

Hans and Catherine Johannsen are pictured around 1910. Hans immigrated in the early 1870s, sponsored by Claus Gottsch, who hired him as a farmhand. He told his grandchildren that Indians still lived in the area when he moved here, and he walked to the Hayes Post Office to get and send mail. He saved up enough to buy passage for his wife, Catherine, to join him. The couple had five children; three survived, one died in infancy, and a son died at the age of 10.

Pictured here from left to right, siblings Henry, Henrietta, and Adoph Mueller emigrated from Germany in 1891 when they were teenagers. Pastor Dierks, their uncle, sponsored them. They lived in Nemaha County for a while before moving to the Bennington area. Once established, they sponsored both their parents, another sister, and two more brothers.

George and Antonie Mangold are pictured around 1905. George was the son of Peter and Mary Mangold. George's mother was the eldest child of the Glandt family, one of the earliest families to settle in Nebraska. His father grew up on a farm near Davenport. The couple married in 1878 and moved to a farm not far from Bennington. They had nine children. George took over his father's jobs, which included merchant, stock and grain buyer, coal dealer, lumberyard proprietor, banker, and elevator owner.

Otto Gottsch (left) and Henry Paulsen (right) represented the first generation born in the Bennington area; both were born in 1877, and both passed away just weeks before their 100th birthdays. Otto was the son of Charles Gottsch, whose family settled here in 1858, and he lived his entire life on the family's homestead. Both had vivid memories of the 1888 blizzard, and Gottsch told stories of how the 1913 tornado destroyed much of his family's farm. He was an official ambassador for the Trans-Mississippi International Exposition, held in Omaha in 1898, and traveled the country promoting the event. He served as president of the Plattdeutsch Verein, managed the Bennington Juvenile Military Band, and served on the school board. Henry Paulsen's parents settled just north of the Gottsch farm. He recalled the School Children's Blizzard of 1888, when the family woke up to snow drifts that nearly covered their home and barn. After digging out of their house, Henry had to climb up a 15-foot snow drift and enter the barn through the upstairs loft window in order to feed their horses. He was active on the school board and served as town marshal. Paulsen started a well digging and drilling business; the rate for digging a well when he started was 35¢ per vertical foot.

Col. James Pratt served in the Union army during the Civil War. After the war, he received a government contract to supply goods to Fort Randall in Dakota Territory and later to Indian reservations in western Nebraska. He started a lucrative freight hauling business out of Sidney, Nebraska, at the time of the Black Hills gold rush. He diversified and invested heavily in land, ranching, and cattle in Wyoming and Texas. He purchased land three miles south of the current site of Bennington in 1879 and built it into a showcase farming estate called Summer Hill Farm. He retired and lived there until his death in 1910. (Courtesy of Weyland Magee.)

Two

Evolution in Farming

Many of the early farmers had little to start with—possibly a horse, a wagon, and a few hand tools. Their best attributes were their willingness to work hard, the ability to adapt and learn, and lastly, their perseverance through good times and bad. They faced droughts, floods, grasshoppers, hail, prairie fires, tornados, blizzards, injury, and even death. Many were sponsored by established settlers who needed farmhands. A few early arrivals had considerable resources to get started by themselves.

A good example was Claus Gottsch and his son Charles, who sponsored several immigrants from their European homeland. Immigrants needed a sponsor who would supply them with a job and a roof over their head and help them with language and other transitional challenges to become a citizen. It was a successful system.

Col. James Pratt, a veteran of the Civil War, purchased land just south of the current site of Bennington in 1879 and began building his Summer Hill Farm estate. When he finished, he had amassed 1,800 acres, and his farm was a showcase of modern agricultural practices.

What farmers accomplished within a century is amazing. The evolution from horse to the internal combustion engine revolutionized agriculture, turning the "Great American Desert" into one of the most productive agricultural regions in the world. That mechanical revolution was filled with ingenuity, imagination, and some failures, but built on successes. Each generation made farming easier and more productive for the next.

Immigrants often left behind family, friends, and most of their belongings to come to America. Many started out with little more than a dream. Land was relatively inexpensive, but the challenge was to establish a livelihood and build a home. Early photographs were often taken of the family posing in front of their homestead. They took great pride in their accomplishment and their new country.

Farmer Roy Gordon is plowing behind a three-horse team. "Sod busting" was terribly hard work for both horses and man. A farmer would have to wrestle a plow a distance of roughly 20 miles over rough and uneven ground to plow 10 acres. Then the ground had to be disked or harrowed before planting. He then faced walking a similar distance to plant by hand, then hoe weeds, and if lucky, walk more to harvest. Early farming was said to be hard on shoe leather.

Here a farmer is using a roller to break up clods and push stones into the ground to make planting and harvesting easier. (Courtesy of Weyland Magee.)

A farmer cuts wheat. This piece of horse-drawn equipment would cut the wheat, and at intervals, it would dump the wheat into a pile that would be later tied together by the farmer forming a sheaf. Several sheaves would be stacked against one other to keep the grain from being on the ground. This formed a shock. The shocks would be collected and the grain separated by thrashing. (Courtesy of Weyland Magee.)

The harvest dictated a major portion if not all of a farming family's income. It was common that everyone in the family participated in the harvest. A crop was a huge investment in seed, equipment, and labor, and it could easily be lost to livestock, grasshoppers, hail, strong winds, or wildfires.

A devastating hail storm went through the Bennington area in 1915. The storm hit on July 18, beating the wheat and oats into the ground and shredding the corn plants. This young man is cultivating what remains of the corn crop. While the crop would not produce corn, the rest of the plant could be partially salvaged by feeding it to cattle. A similar storm hit in 1917. (Courtesy of Weyland Magee.)

A farmhand foolishly attempted to cross a flooded creek with a wagon full of corn. His attempt led to disaster: a wagon stuck axle-deep in mud and a horse down. Whether from slipping, injury or even fatigue, having a horse go down was serious business. A horse could easily cause itself more injury or hurt its teammate trying to get up.

This thrashing machine was powered by a steam tractor. Shocks of grain were collected and hauled in from the field and were fed into the thrasher by pitchfork. The thrasher separated the grain from the chaff. The grain is being augured into the wagon, and the straw is being blown to the left. Straw was normally collected and used for livestock bedding.

The J.L. Case Thrashing Machine Company was one of the first manufactures to offer farmers power on wheels. These tractors were massive and slow-moving machines. Power output of this steam engine was roughly 25 horsepower. It pulled a cart that held extra fuel and water for the boiler. The large wheel just ahead of the driver was a flywheel that powered equipment such as thrashing machines, sawmills, and grinders. Power was transferred from the tractor by the use of a long drive belt. The roof protected the driver from hot embers and smoke from the smoke stack.

Col. James Pratt's home at Summer Hill Farm is pictured here. The colonel purchased the land in 1879, and by the time of his death in 1910, the estate consisted of 1,800 acres. He used the property as a summer estate to escape the city but eventually lived there fulltime. He was president of the Anchor Fence Company and director of the Union Stockyards in south Omaha. (Courtesy of Weyland Magee.)

The main building complex at Summer Hill Farm is pictured in 1910. Not many barns in the country flew the American flag. From left to right are a two-story corn crib, granary, horse barn, water plant, and the foreman's living quarters. The large barn was necessary to house the nearly 40 horses needed to farm. (Courtesy of Weyland Magee.)

Summer Hill Farm was a large operation and during the field season needed a crew of 20 men. This required a minimum of 20 teams of horses and explains the large barn and granary. The majority of the oats crop was fed to the horses. Workers were paid around $4 a day, and a skilled "husker" could pick 100 bushels of eared corn a day. (Courtesy of Weyland Magee.)

Here is a beautiful field of oat shocks. This was the first step in harvesting; next came the task of thrashing. (Courtesy of Weyland Magee.)

This is a Case 10-20 kerosene tractor. The model came out in 1915 and boasted a 10-horsepower rating at its drawbar and 20 horsepower at its flywheel. Many of these early powered engines started on gasoline; once they had warmed up, the fuel was switched to less expensive diesel oil. (Courtesy of Weyland Magee.)

This is the furrow left behind by a three-bottom plow being pulled by a Case 10-20 tractor. This plow had three blades or "bottoms" that cut and then flipped the soil upside down. This broke up the soil, making it easier to till and plant. (Courtesy of Weyland Magee.)

This farmer is filling the seed corn hoppers of his two-row planter around 1936. The tractor is a John Deere Model B pulling a John Deere planter. Horse-drawn equipment was often modified with a tongue that could attach to the tractor's drawbar. The conversion from horses to tractors was easy. (Courtesy of Weyland Magee.)

Enno Mueller and his son Gordon are posing with their new Allis-Chalmers tractors around 1955. Allis-Chalmers offered the first tractor mounted on rubber tires. Tractor manufacturers were known for their distinctive colors. Allis-Chalmers equipment was bright orange, John Deeres bright green and yellow, Fords gray, and Farmalls bright red. (Author's collection.)

A 1914 Ford Model T runabout is being used to check Summer Hill Farm fields. Henry Ford made 15.5 million Model Ts that put America on wheels. The car had 22.5 horsepower, and with chains, could go almost anywhere. (Courtesy of Weyland Magee.)

Henry Dornacker is pictured with a full load of corn. This wagon is set up for husking on the left side. Dornacker's team was trained to walk only as fast as he could pick corn by hand. The tall sideboard is a "bang board," which prevented tossed ears from flying over the wagon. A good husker could pick 100 bushels of corn a day.

The crew at Summer Hill Farm is unloading a wagon of eared corn. A wagon lift raised the front of the wagon so the corn would slide out the tailgate and into the elevator, where it was conveyed into a bin. Otherwise, it had to be scooped by shovel. (Courtesy of Weyland Magee.)

This is the corn drying room at Summer Hill Farm. The best ears of corn were selected at harvest, allowed to dry, and then shelled and used for seed the following spring. Seed corn companies began offering hardier hybrid varieties in the 1950s, which replaced this method of acquiring seed. (Courtesy of Weyland Magee.)

Roy Gordon is holding his little piggy, and both look quite content. A good farmer was always concerned about the health of his livestock. Hogs were often fed eared corn; they ate the grain but left the cob behind. A common farm chore of smaller children was to gather those cobs for their mother's cook stove. The heat generated from corn cobs provided many a cooked meal and also heated homes.

Charles Gottsch is driving a herd of cattle down Warehouse Street. Farmers shipped and received livestock on the railroad. Livestock pens were on the west end of town, but stock was loaded and unloaded east of the depot. Livestock was common in Bennington during the early 1900s. Many town families had small barns where they kept their horse, a few chickens, and possibly even a hog or two.

Duane Braesch and Roland Sass had a trucking and corn-shelling business. Earned corn was fed into the sheller, which produced three products. Here, cobs are being dropped on the pile on the left, corn shucks are being blown out the tube, and corn is being augured into the wagon. Shucks and cobs were often used for livestock bedding. (Courtesy of Weyland Magee.)

Arnold Mueller is seen here feeding his hogs around 1925. Cattle, sheep, and horses would generally be put out to graze in a pasture and provided water. However, some livestock, such as hogs and chickens, normally required daily attention.

Nancy Oft poses with a calf. Many farm children practiced animal husbandry in 4-H clubs. Oft had a fascination with animals, but it was practiced through her painting. She would take the train to Fremont, where she took painting lessons. The round-trip fare was 40¢. Oft was a prolific artist when she married Roy Gordon. The couple's first child, Douglas, tragically died a few hours after birth. The trauma was so great that Nancy never picked up a paint brush again. Unfortunately, many families lost children in those days.

Hundreds of pieces of wood and shingles are being arranged to construct Lester Logemann's barn. Anyone can build a pitched roof, but it takes skill to build a rounded one. This barn was erected in 1946, just after World War II. (Courtesy of Coe Leta Logemann.)

Ford Model Ts were dependable and adaptable. Here, Charles Heise has set his car's rear axle on a block and is using his rear tire rim and a belt to power a pump jack that is pumping water from his well. (Courtesy of Dale Logemann.)

Roy Gordon holds a prized lavender mink he helped develop through breeding. The pink-colored animal became world renowned and popular in the fashion industry. Minks have a great set of teeth that is their primary means of defense, and getting bit was an occupational hazard. Gordon always carried a bottle of iodine to treat wounds, but the treatment often hurt as bad as the bite.

Roy Gordon's mink ranch was a half mile west of Bennington. Gordon started raising minks in the backyard of his Bennington home in 1940, but he soon moved the operation out to the family farm. Operations expanded, and by 1960, his mink herd had reached 5,000, each requiring its own cage.

It takes a lot of hay to feed livestock through the winter, and that required a great deal of work to grow and to store it. These farmers are unloading and transferring hay to the hay loft, which had a track that could hoist hay up and transfer it horizontally inside the loft.

Manure accumulated during winter months and when farmers were busy planting and harvesting crops. When time permitted, it had to be hauled out to the fields in a manure spreader. This was a specialized wagon with a conveyor that would slide the manure into a set of spinning blades that would scatter it behind the wagon. However, drivers were not immune to being hit with a little fertilizer themselves.

A farm family poses in a two-wheel cart. Two-wheeled carts carried a lighter load than a wagon and required only one horse rather than a team to pull them. Early Mormon pioneers used a smaller version to carry their belongings that was pulled by hand. The families pushed or pulled their carts on their walk to Utah.

Elvin Hoier is shown here picking corn. Machinery created safety hazards, and if one looks closely, Hoier has a prosthetic hook for a right hand. While attempting to unplug a corn picker, his hand was pulled in and crushed by the picker's rollers. A farmhand was unable to free him, and his hand had to be amputated by Dr. C.W. Hickey. Farm-related accidents and deaths were far too common. (Courtesy of Sandra Japp.)

Larry (left) and Darrell Logemann pose on their dad's Ford tractor. It wasn't unusual for farm boys in their early teens to drive tractors and even pickups to help their fathers. This was especially true during harvest, when additional help was needed. (Courtesy of Coe Leta Logemann.)

SnowCo manufacturing on McKinley Street invented a bale thrower that attached to a truck. The truck driver guided the bale into a loading slot, which triggered a clamp that grabbed the bale and lifted it up to the loaders. It allowed a crew of only two men to effectively load a truck with bales. (Courtesy of Coe Leta Logemann.)

Farmers check the bin for wheat on an early Minneapolis Moline pull-type combine. These combines revolutionized grain harvest. Instead of having four distinct harvest phases—cutting, binding sheaves, gathering, and thrashing—the combine accomplished all with one single pass. These time-saving machines allowed farmers to increase the acreage they farmed.

Rural living had its challenges, especially when it came to travel. Poor roads, inadequate drainage, and spring thaw often made the simplest trip to town impossible. Buggies, wagons, and the automobile simply could not navigate axle-deep mud. Road improvement projects began in earnest in the 1920s. Country roads were elevated and constructed with proper ditches and drainage, and road tops received gravel and routine maintenance.

Three

The Railroad and Bennington

The Fremont, Elkhorn & Missouri Valley Railroad acquired a rail corridor from Fremont to north Omaha in 1868. It had constructed a line from Missouri Valley, Iowa, to Fremont and was planning to build a connecting line to Omaha. However, in 1887, the Chicago & Northwestern Railroad purchased those rights and began laying track from Bell Creek (Arlington) south toward Irvington.

The Pioneer Townsite Company was affiliated with the railroad, and identified and surveyed new townsites along the line. On this particular connection, it planned the new towns of Washington and Bennington and changed the name of Bell Creek to Arlington. It is interesting that the names of all four towns—Arlington, Washington, Bennington, and Irvington—end in "-ington."

Tracks reached the proposed townsite of Washington first, and it was dedicated in September 1887. Bennington followed two months later, on November 15. The Hayes Post Office was moved to Washington and the Blakely Post Office to Bennington, since mail was now being delivered by train rather than by horse or stagecoach. City lots went on sale and construction began in 1887. These communities grew rapidly, allowing Bennington to incorporate in 1892; Washington followed in 1915. The Bennington Village Board of Trustees was elected and had its first meeting on April 15, 1892. City government was officially born.

The railroad and these villages sustained each other for nearly a century. Trains hauled in the building materials, equipment, and laborers necessary to construct the towns, as well as the merchandise that stocked the shelves when businesses opened. Economic development spread to the countryside as farms became more numerous and expanded, with more livestock and larger crops. The railroad was also key to getting farm products to market. That mutual reliance began to change with the arrival of the first horseless carriage. Automobiles largely replaced the need for passenger service after World War II, and the growth in the trucking industry eventually made shipping on the Arlington-to-Irvington rail line unprofitable.

A runaway brush fire in the early 1970s burned a nearby railroad bridge. Faced with the cost of replacement, the railroad chose instead to simply abandon the line. The rails and ties and infrastructure were pulled out, and unfortunately, the depot was burned by the fire department for training purposes.

The Fremont, Elkhorn & Missouri Valley Railroad planned a shortcut between Fremont and north Omaha. The Chicago & Northwestern Railroad took over that project and started laying track in 1887. The plan included creating two new towns, Bennington and Washington, and renaming Bell Creek Arlington. That line ran from Arlington through Washington and Bennington to Irvington.

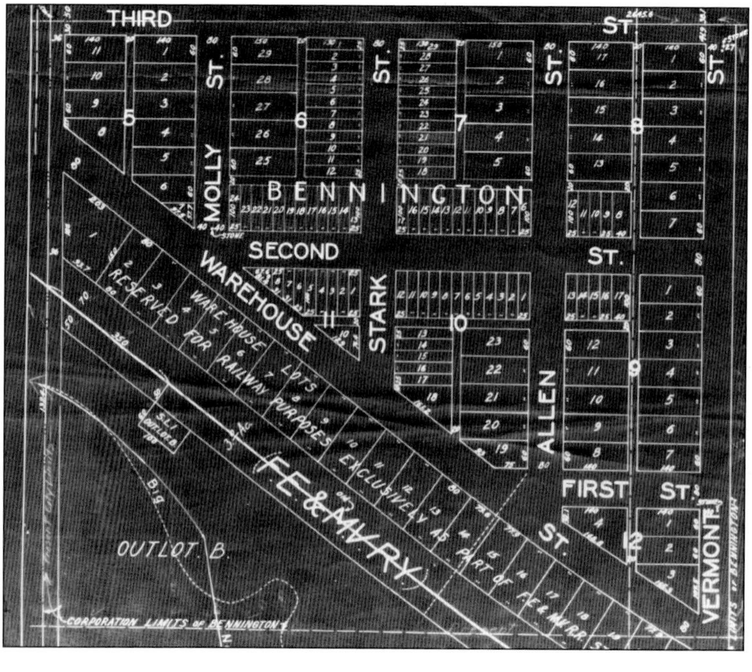

This is the initial town plat the Pioneer Townsite Company developed before the Fremont, Elkhorn & Missouri Valley Railroad sold out. The town was named after the Revolutionary War battle of Bennington, Vermont. Stark and Allen Streets were named for the generals who led that battle. The townsite of Bennington was dedicated on November 15, 1887.

The Pioneer Town Site Company offered lots for sale beginning in 1887. Eggert Oft invested in nine lots, all within two blocks of the depot. He first built a hotel where his family could live. Oft's Hotel also contained a saloon and social hall. With that completed, he went on to build a livery stable, harness shop, blacksmith shop, and large icehouse behind his hotel and saloon.

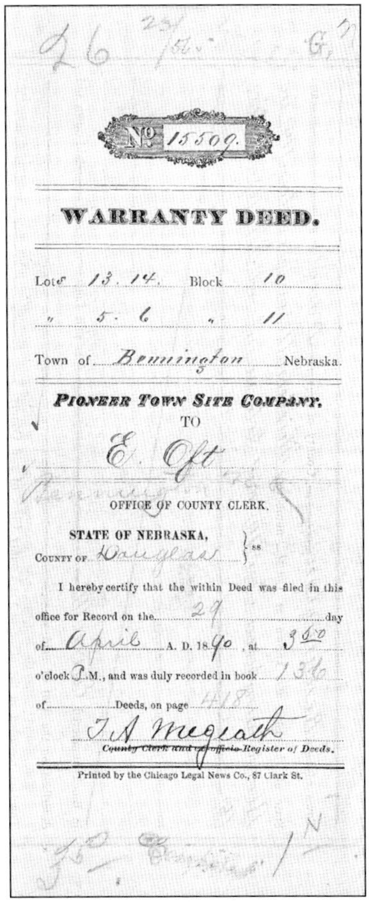

No. 15509.

WARRANTY DEED.

Lots 13. 14. Block 10
" 5. 6 " 11

Town of Bennington Nebraska.

PIONEER TOWN SITE COMPANY,

TO

E. Oft

OFFICE OF COUNTY CLERK.

STATE OF NEBRASKA, County of Douglas } ss

I hereby certify that the within Deed was filed in this office for Record on the 29 day of April A. D. 1890, at 3 50 o'clock P.M., and was duly recorded in book 136 of Deeds, on page 418.

T. A. Megeath
County Clerk and Ex-officio Register of Deeds.

Printed by the Chicago Legal News Co., 87 Clark St.

The baggage truck crew is waiting for the next train to arrival at the Bennington Depot. The Chicago & Northwestern Railroad ran a maximum of six daily trains (three east and three west) between Fremont and Omaha. They passed (east) through Arlington, Washington, Bennington, Irvington, and Omaha. Fare between those towns was about a penny per mile in 1910.

A storm on January 12, 1888, is known as the School Children's Blizzard. Nearly 300 children lost their lives attempting to get home from school in the hurricane-force winds and blinding snow. A telegraph attendant in a sidecar at the Irvington station feared for his life but found his way to the depot by dragging his foot along the rail and reaching out every few steps to find the loading platform. Although it was impossible to see in the storm, he felt his way to shelter and safety.

Section Chief Baker's crew poses in front of his headquarters and residence on the outskirts of Bennington. It was Baker's responsibility to check and maintain the tracks in his district. A lot of the work centered around inspecting the tracks by handcar and replacing rotting or loose rail ties.

This is Baker's home surrounded by floodwaters in 1916. Papio Creek ran behind the home and frequently flooded. The Army Corp of Engineers started a flood control project in the 1930s that deepened and straightened the creek. That increased water velocity, and the creek naturally eroded itself a deeper channel. This increased channel capacity and reduced flooding.

The valley was prone to flooding during spring thaw and after heavy rains. This photograph was taken from George Mangold's elevator tower looking west. In the background to the left is Oft's grist mill, and moving across the tracks to the right one can see Hans and Henry Schneider's saloon.

This is a northwest view of the Mangold Elevator overlooking the intersection of Molley, South Second, and Warehouse Streets. The Mangold Brothers lumberyard is in the foreground; the large two-story building across the street is the Edelweiss Inn. Henry and Bertha Jipp's farm is in the background.

This 1910 photograph was taken from the elevator loft and shows the rear of businesses on the south side of South Second Street. From left to right are George Mangold's store, Pete Petersen's meat shop, Henry Schroeder's harness shop, and Oft's Hotel. Petersen butchered animals in the back of his shop. Across the street, from left to right, are Gustav Paulson's blacksmith shop, Otto Hansen's meat shop, and, hidden behind the trees, the Bennington House and Storz Saloon.

This view from the Mangold Elevator looks northeast across Stark Street. Bert Seymour's blacksmith shop is in the foreground, across the street is George Ohrt and C.W. Glandt's hardware store and office, and the large building on the hill is the Modern Woodmen of America hall.

Oft's livery stable was one block north of the railroad station. The stable was built shortly after 1888 and burned in the 1913 fire. (Courtesy of Bonnie Mangold.)

A Chicago & Northwestern Railroad crew assesses a breakdown. The Arlington-to-Irvington line had a single set of tracks and only had side tracks near the depots. Either repairs had to be made on the spot or locomotives and cars had to be towed to repair shops in Omaha before traffic could resume.

A railroad crew is hard at work building a sturdier bridge next to the original one. Large stone blocks are being placed as footings using a timber crane and steam-driven windlass.

Herman Timme is believed to have built the first store in 1887, but it was west of 156th Street and just outside city limits. It also housed Bennington's first post office. Timme served as Bennington's justice of the peace in 1892. He conducted the first official census when the town was hosting sugar beet harvesters and railroad workers. This was done to ensure his count exceeded the 100 needed for Bennington to officially meet the requirement for incorporation. (Courtesy of the Zion Evangelical Lutheran Church.)

This aerial photograph was taken of Bennington in 1959. The large diagonal street on the left is South Second Street, and the one on the right is Warehouse Street. The railroad tracks can be seen running parallel to Warehouse Street at far right. Bennington Park was out of view to the right of the tracks.

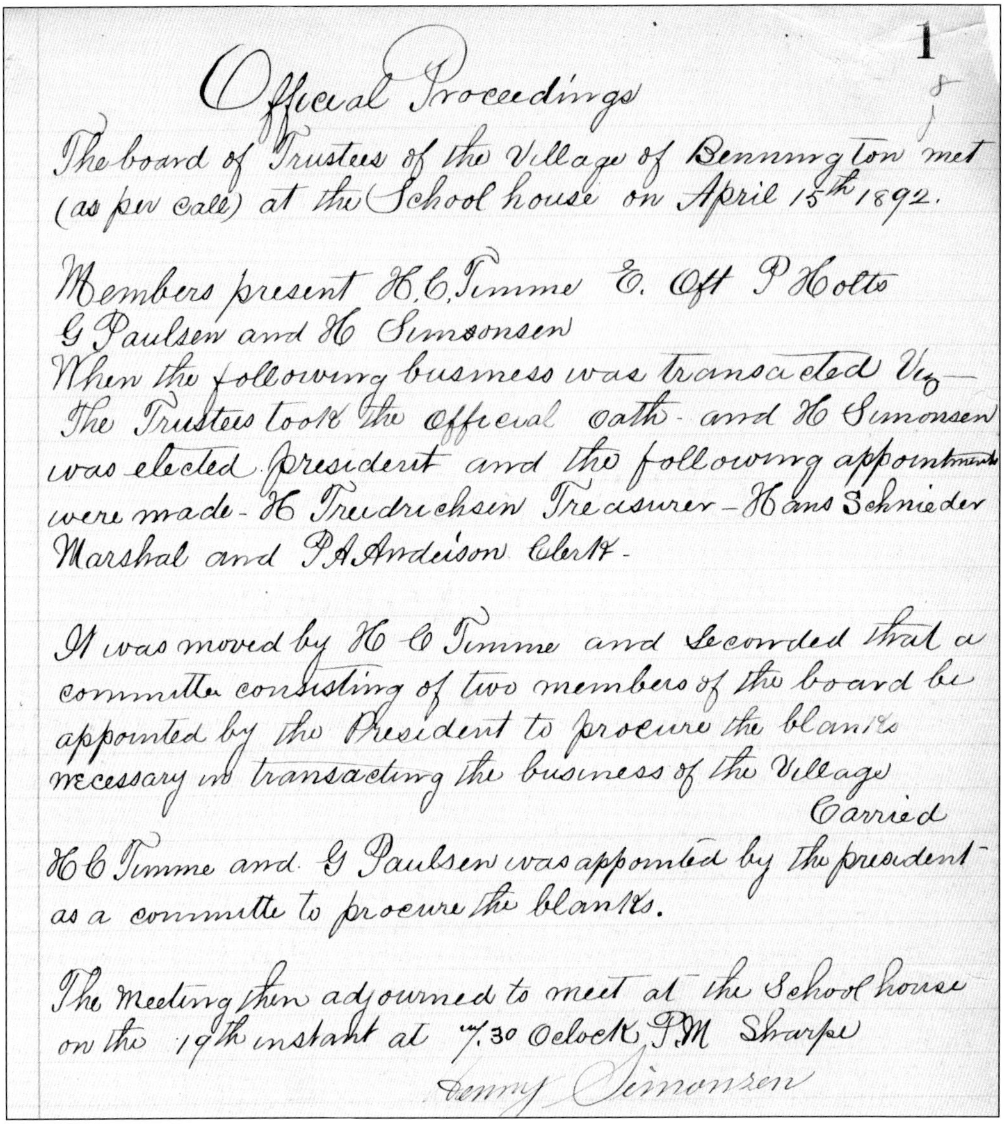
1

Offical Proceedings

The board of Trustees of the Village of Bennington met (as per call) at the School house on April 15th 1892.

Members present H. C. Timme E. Oft P Holts G Paulsen and H Simonsen
When the following business was transacted Viz—
The Trustees took the offical oath - and H Simonsen was elected president and the following appointments were made - H Friedrichsen Treasurer - Hans Schnieder Marshal and P.A. Anderson Clerk -

It was moved by H C Timme and Seconded that a committee consisting of two members of the board be appointed by the President to procure the blanks necessary in transacting the business of the Village
Carried

H C Timme and G Paulsen was appointed by the president as a committe to procure the blanks.

The meeting then adjourned to meet at the School house on the 19th instant at 7.30 Oclock P.M Sharpe

Henry Simonsen

Henry Simonsen's handwritten minutes record the first meeting (April 15, 1892) of the Bennington Board of Trustees. Board members included Hy Simonsen, Eggert Oft, Gustav Paulsen, Herman Timme, and Peter Holst.

Four

Business and Street Views

Construction began in the fall of 1887, but railroad track layers did not finish until the end of the year. Building really got started the following spring, when materials could be delivered by rail. In less than five years, the village had four saloons, two hotels, and several stores and small businesses. Construction even spilled outside of the proposed city limits onto land owned by Claus Oft. He sold lots across the western boundary of the new town that were brought into the city limits during incorporation in 1892.

Wood was the primary construction material, although some of the roofs in the business district were metal. Bricks were used sparingly in foundations due to their expense. Conditions were primitive by today's standards. There was no indoor plumbing, and homes and businesses used outhouses. Buildings were heated by potbellied stoves, and light came from coal oil lanterns and carbide gas. The mixture of wood and open flame proved disastrous.

The business community experienced two major fires, one in 1911 and the second in 1913. The first destroyed Mangold's store, Petersen's meat shop, and Schroeder's harness shop. The second destroyed nearly half the business district and several barns and even caught the church roof on fire. Claus Glandt and Tim Ohrt started manufacturing cement blocks around this time, and builders started using block and brick to rebuild. These fires also triggered a serious attempt to establish a volunteer fire department. However, the challenge for half a century was how to pay for expensive equipment. That was remedied in 1962, when Nebraska passed legislation creating rural fire districts that had their own taxation authority.

The Bennington community was fairly self-sufficient by the 1920s. It had two grocery stores, a large lumberyard, a farmer's union, two banks, four saloons, a livery, a harness and shoe shop, a grain elevator, a hotel, two hardware stores, a cigar factory, two churches, a barbershop, a meat shop, a gristmill, a bakery, two social halls, a school, a newspaper, a doctor, a veterinarian, and train service.

Starting in the mid-1920s, the state's highway and road development programs arrived in the community with improvements to the area roads and the creation of Highway 36 through town. That made travel by automobile much more efficient.

Some businessmen wanted to be first and did not wait for the Pioneer Town Site Company to sell lots. Bennington's first store (around 1886) was operated by Felix Ebner from a tent just east of 156th Street. When lots were sold, Ebner purchased one and moved. Claus Oft sold land adjacent to the proposed town. Bennington's first permanent structure was Herman Timme's store, which was adjacent to the proposed city limits. It was built in 1887 and also housed the village's first post office.

The Oft grist mill weir provided the elevation difference necessary to turn the waterwheel that powered the mill's grinder. Farmers brought their wheat and corn to be ground into flour and meal. The mill's pond also provided fishing, hunting, swimming, and boating opportunities to the community. The mill operated until 1926.

Here is a view of the Oft grist mill looking east during spring thaw. The mill pond would freeze over in the winter, and when it reached a sufficient thickness, men would harvest the ice. Ice blocks were cut with hand saws, pulled out, and stacked in icehouses to be used in the summer.

The Mangold Brothers lumber company is shown here. The Mangold brothers sold their business to the Christensen Lumber Company in Fremont, which operated the business for a few years before selling to Harry Miles in 1937. Harry and his son Don Miles ran the business until 1940, when Don bought out his father and ran the business with his son Jerry Miles.

Oft's Hotel was on the southwest corner of South Second and Stark Streets. Built by Eggert Oft in 1888, it housed a hotel, saloon, and social hall. The Oft family lived there. The town had dug a cistern in the center of the intersection. Here, Volunteer Hose Company No. 1 tests its hand pump wagon. The company's equipment consisted of the hand pump, a ladder, and 50 buckets for a water brigade.

Margaretha Petersen and her children are standing in front of their family's meat shop in Bennington. This photograph was taken in the early 1900s. Early settlers were predominately from Schleswig-Holstein, the two northern provinces of Germany. The sign proclaims that fact: *Fleesch Laden* is German for "meat store." The Petersens offered a variety of German sausages and other delicacies.

Margaretha Petersen is working behind the counter of the family meat shop. Hams and sausages hang from the walls along with hind and front quarters of beef. It was probably necessary to butcher nearly every day in order to offer fresh meat. Meat could be held for a day or two in ice boxes, but without refrigeration or freezers, the only long-term methods of preservation were curing with salt, smoking, drying, canning, and even pickling.

August Witte's hardware store was on the northwest corner of Stark and South Second Streets. It was built in 1888 and also had a connecting barn on the north end that initially served as a mortuary. Records show that embalming was an optional service.

Dr. C.W. Hickey was Bennington's doctor for 50 years. Here, Dr. Hickey and his team are ready to make a house call. When it was snowy, his buggy was replaced with a light enclosed sleigh, which was easier for the horses to pull and more comfortable for him. Changing with the times, he bought a horseless carriage when they first came out. He found it emotionally difficult to part with his team; it had safely delivered him on his routes through rain, sleet, and hail for 10 years. He would soon discover his horses were far more dependable.

Village employees are grading the ruts out of Stark Street with an eight-horse team. Paving streets did not begin until 1924. The building on the left is August Witte's hardware store. The barn to the right of the mortuary and behind the horses is believed to have been the town's veterinarian office at one time.

The inside of Bert Seymour's blacksmith shop was similar to many others of the day. Seymour repaired and sold wooden-spoked wheels, shoed horses, welded, and fixed nearly anything. The bare-chested man next to the anvil is probably Seymour.

The Friedrichsen family operated a store on the southeast corner of Stark and South Second Streets. The family had five daughters. The store sold lunch, bulk groceries, canned goods, cigarettes, cigars, and root beer and other beverages. It fell victim to the 1913 fire.

Henry Arp and his family are standing in front of his implement dealership, which was south of the intersection of Molley and Warehouse Streets. The lots between Warehouse Street and the railroad tracks were reserved for businesses dealing in heavy and bulky cargo. Arp sold Deering, Canton, and other brands of farm equipment. In later years, the Bunz family and Chet Witte took over the business.

Henry and Clarence Paulsen are digging a new well for Weyland Magee in 1934. Henry's father, Gustav Paulsen, emigrated from Germany in 1875. He opened a blacksmith shop in Washington but later dismantled both his home and barn and moved them to Bennington. (Courtesy of Weyland Magee.)

One of the first businesses to open was the hardware store on the northwest corner of Stark and South Second Streets. It was built by Hy Simonsen and a Mr. Schnidt. It was later owned by Chris Steinert, J.H. Siert, and then August Witte, who also became the community's mortician and funeral director. Witte operated the store until 1917, when he sold out. He remained the town's funeral director until Bill Haden became the mortician in 1934.

Jefferson's was one of two large stores in Washington. This photograph was taken around the late 1920s. (Courtesy of Loren Cohrs.)

Post offices were generally inside stores, taking up a small area of the business. Sometimes, they were in a wing of a building or even in someone's home. This was the Washington Post Office in 1930. (Courtesy of Loren Cohrs.)

A salesman is attentively waiting to make a sale. Tobacco products were far more popular at the turn of the 20th century than today. George Scheef had learned the trade of making cigars in Germany and opened a store in Bennington featuring cigars. This c. 1913 image is believed to have been taken either in Scheef's shop or a local saloon.

Henry and Hans Schneider built the first saloon in Bennington west of 156th Street, next to the railroad tracks. The saloon was built outside of the proposed townsite on land purchased from Claus Oft. Hans Schneider was the first city marshal, and is believed to be the man at right wearing the badge.

Nielsen's general merchandise and meat market was in Washington and is pictured around the 1930s. Both Washington and Bennington began to lose their retail stores by the 1960s when it became routine to go to Benson or Omaha to shop. Small-town merchants simply could not compete with larger stores for selection or price. (Courtesy of Loren Cohrs.)

The 1911 fire destroyed Schroeder's harness shop, and in its place, Eggert Oft constructed one of the first brick buildings in town. It housed the Bennington State Bank. Both the Bennington State Bank and the Mangold and Glandt Bank fell victim to the agricultural depression of the 1920s and closed during the 1928 bank panic.

Bennington's South Second Street is seen looking east on a busy day in 1913. The automobile was making its appearance. A banner at the far end of the street announces a Saturday baseball game at Bennington Park.

John Petersen had a prosperous garage business. He sold six varieties of cars that could be ordered and delivered by train. Petersen was the first to put electric lights in his shop; they were powered by a small generator and batteries. Neighboring businesses were impressed, and before long, Petersen was providing them electric power too. The city board approached him with the proposition that it would loan him the money to buy a larger generator if he would supply power to the entire city. He did. The first power service did not continue through the night, as there was not enough demand to make it profitable. Petersen powered the generator down 15 minutes before he shut it off, and this brownout signaled customers that it was time to light their oil lamps or they would be left in the dark.

Metz Brothers was the first brewery established in Omaha and one of its first manufacturers, opening for business in 1859. Grothusen's Saloon in Bennington served Metz beer until it burned in 1913. The saloon was rebuilt and operated by the Paulsen family. The location of this bar could not be determined.

Fred Kruse (left) is behind the bar of the newly constructed Storz Saloon in 1914. The 1913 fire destroyed the first Storz Saloon and the adjoining Bennington House hotel. The Storz Brewery rebuilt the saloon, but not the hotel. Beer has been served here for more than 130 years.

An automobile rally gathers in front of Bert Seymour's blacksmith shop in 1907. Seymour was one of the first to recognize the transition from horses to the automobile. The arrival of cars caused a stir in society. They offered independence and greater mobility, but these new machines were prone to breakdowns, and venturing out into the country by oneself could be risky. Touring clubs helped solve that issue, and it also proved more fun to travel in groups.

Peter "Doc" and Hazel Christiansen settled in Bennington in 1922. They came from Denmark, where Peter was a veterinarian. He started a practice in Bennington and Boy's Town specializing in farm animals, especially horses. The couple had two children, Betty and Charles. Charles enlisted in the Coast Guard in 1943 and became a naval pilot who served in both World War II and Korea.

George Mangold and his family are standing in front of their store. The store was built in 1898 on the corner of South Second and Warehouse Streets. The couple offered a wide range of groceries and housewares. What they did not have could be ordered and delivered by train in a few days.

George Mangold relocated across the street after the 1911 fire destroyed his business. He built one of the first brick and cement block buildings on a lot that originally had a small blacksmith shop. Tim Ohrt had started a cement block fabrication business off Warehouse Street. Years later, the store housed the Bennington Post Office. George, Walter Mangold, and later Leonard Mangold all served as postmaster.

This view of the northeast corner of Stark and South Second Streets shows, from left to right, the Mangold and Glandt Bank, Hagedorn and Ohrt's furniture store and post office, a pool hall, a meat market, a cigar shop, and the Modern Woodmen of America hall. The photograph was taken sometime between 1914 and 1924. (Courtesy of Corey Olsberg.)

Final touches are being made to Oft's Hall in 1914. Eggert Oft replaced Oft's Hotel with two buildings: a smaller structure that was operated by John Petersen as a grocery store and a two-story building that was a social hall. The downstairs had a kitchen, restaurant, bar, and pool hall, while a large dance floor and two stages graced the upstairs. It became a popular destination for social functions.

Calendars have been a popular mode of advertising for more than a century. The main goal has always been to use illustrations or photographs that catch the eye. This calendar was destined for the garage or someone's shop rather than mother's kitchen.

C.W. Glandt had a hardware and farm supply store on Stark Street. Glandt was a leading businessman in town and was involved in several businesses. He sold insurance, operated the pool hall, started a concrete block business, and was heavily involved in home construction. He and his son built over 100 homes in the community.

John Petersen was quite an entrepreneur in several different business ventures. He managed a grocery store after 1914 and later opened a garage farther down the block. Along with being a salesman and mechanic, he is credited with introducing electric power to Bennington. Years later, he manufactured electric door openers.

The Mangold and Glandt Bank is pictured with (from left to right) John, George, and Peter Mangold. The original bank was built by James Valnack and Vernon Wallace in 1888. Wolly and Stratton bought the bank in 1894 and operated it for one year before selling to Peter Mangold and C.W. Glandt. They operated from this building until 1914, when they built a new and larger bank farther down the block.

Anna Short Harrington, dressed as her character Aunt Jemima, is posing with the staff from the Clover Farm Store. The photograph was taken during World War II, when Quaker Oats was promoting the brand by hosting pancake feeds. Quaker Oats had the distinction of having the first living trademark. Those remembering the event said that Harrington made the feed a lot of fun.

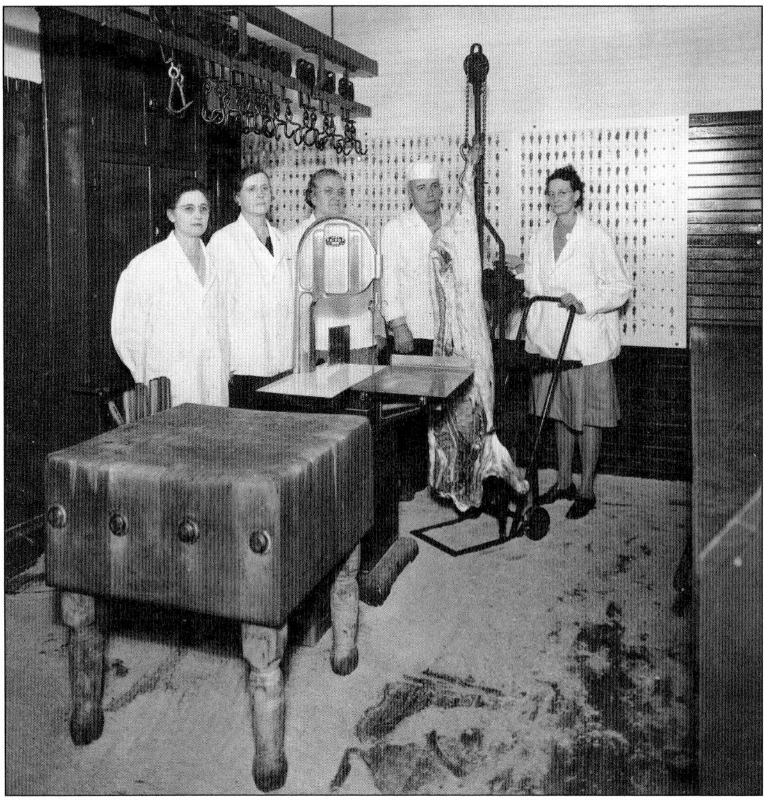

The Clover Farm Store was operated by Roy and Nancy Gordon. Roy had installed a freezer plant and rented out freezer boxes to customers. The rack behind them held the customers' keys to those boxes. The store provided a full assortment of meats and groceries.

Jacob Sass is showing Eggert Oft his flowers. Jacob, Hans, and Henry Sass became world-renowned plant breeders. The American Iris Society honored their achievement in developing irises by creating the Hans and Jacob Sass Medal for the annual winner of the society's intermediate bearded iris contest.

William Musel opened Bill's Hi-Way Service in 1951 on the corner of 156th Street and Highway 36, right across the street from the school. It was a great location to get gas or have one's car worked on, and it was a popular place for students to get a soda or candy bar. Ten years later, Musel moved his business a block west behind his home and operated it with his two sons, Robert and Richard. (Courtesy of Lois Musel.)

Kenneth Nelson started Nelson Produce in 1944. He initially bought eggs, poultry, and cream from farmers for the Omaha market. His business expanded into selling products to farmers. He hired Russell Johns as manager, and Johns purchased the business in 1959 after Nelson's death in an automobile accident. Russel and Doris Johns are shown here. The business was in the building constructed by James Valnack and Vernon Wallace in 1888. (Courtesy of Dean Johns.)

A single-lane iron bridge was placed over the Large Papillion (Papio) Creek west of town in 1908. Approaching buggies and motorized vehicles had to yield to those already on the bridge. Years later, an intoxicated driver hit one of the bridge supports with such force that the entire bridge collapsed. Police found the driver asleep and unhurt in his car, tangled in the wreckage.

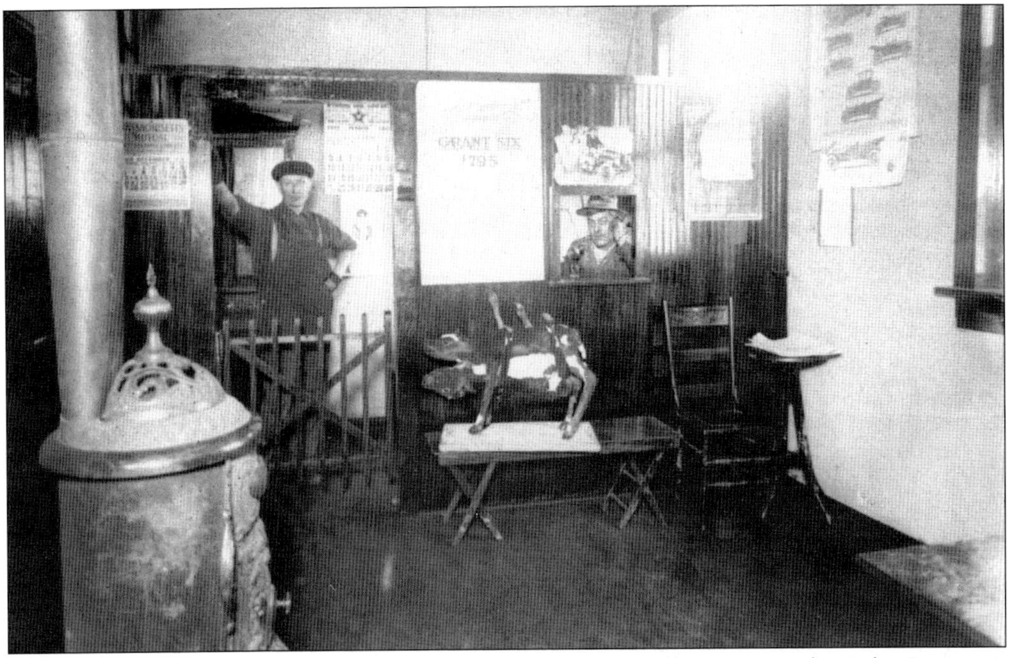

Fred Kniep (standing) and John Petersen (talking on the phone) are pictured in John Petersen's garage around 1920. Petersen built a large two-story building where his brother's meat market burned in 1911. The horseless carriage had arrived in Bennington, and he saw a business opportunity.

The Farmer's Union Co-op and Mercantile Company was initially located at the old elevator by the tracks. When it burned, the co-op moved into the building that had been vacated by the Hagedorn and Ohrt store during the Depression. This photograph was taken in the early 1950s, when the business was managed by Herbert Gottsch and later by George Andersen. It sold farm supplies, equipment, bulk fuel, livestock feed, and coal, and also bought grain. (Courtesy of Melvin Tiedje.)

Hans Neumeyer started and operated Bennington Transfer for more than three decades. He specialized in hauling farm produce to Omaha and bringing back groceries and supplies. Trucks also hauled milk, livestock, grain, and hay. Neumeyer could help with anything that needed to be hauled. (Courtesy of Melvin Tiedje.)

This wreck involved a horse and carriage and automobile. Roads were narrow and usually rutted, and accidents were not uncommon. Horses were skittish and unpredictable when they were confronted with these noisy and smelly machines.

Marion and Herington were photographers who worked the Bennington area. They traveled among the smaller towns taking photographs. Here, bartender Edward Houman is posing with Charles Glandt. Charles and his wife, Minna, came over from Germany in 1892. They became longtime residents and celebrated their 71st wedding anniversary with the community.

The Edelweiss Inn (later the Koch Hotel) was on the northeast corner of Molley and South Second Streets. It was a large two-story structure built in 1897 by Al Schneider. The front of the house was the Edelweiss Saloon, which served Edelweiss beer. Behind the saloon was a dining room that served meals. Upstairs were a bowling lane and hotel rooms. There was a small building behind the hotel where a Dutchman made wooden shoes. The shoes were noisy, but popular.

Bartenders John (left) and Henry Mueller are serving their patrons in a saloon originally bought by the Joseph Schlitz brewing company. A competitor, Gottlieb Storz, purchased a lot and built a saloon farther down the street. There were two other saloons in town: Grothusen's and the Edelweiss Inn. (Courtesy of John Mueller.)

Chester Witte built the Ideal Gas Station in 1928. The station attendant would fill the glass cylinder on top of the pump with gas. The cylinder was calibrated like a rain gauge. When it reached the amount requested, he shut off the pump and drained the gas into the customer's tank using the hose and nozzle. John Petersen's garage is next door.

Bennington's first elevator was built by Peter Diedricksen in 1889 and was operated by a steam engine; unfortunately, it burned down. Peter Mangold rebuilt it but had it powered by a horse on a treadmill. It was on a side track west of the depot. Farmers sold their grain at the elevator, where they unloaded their wagons. The horse-powered conveyor lifted the grain into bins from which it could later be gravity-fed into freight cars for delivery.

This is a view looking east to the Large Papillion Creek and Bennington from Bennington Road. Initially, the road followed the creek. The state straightened the trail to correspond with the section boundary, and this road eventually became State Highway 36. The highway was relocated north of town in the early 1970s.

Many of those who initially settled the Bennington area came from Schleswig-Holstein. It was not uncommon to overhear a conversation or find signs written in German. This is a poster announcing a dance at Eggert Oft's establishment in 1896. A column in the *Bennington Herald* entitled "News from Fatherland" was also in German.

Five

Schools and Churches

One of the first ordinances passed by the city board was to set the cost of an annual liquor license at $500. Those funds were earmarked for Bennington's first school. There were four saloons in town in 1892, and two board members were saloon owners. Some suggest Bennington grew faster than Washington because Washington's liquor license fee was more than twice as much ($1,100) as Bennington's.

The first and second school were on the highest spot in Bennington, on North Second Street between Molley and Stark Streets. However, there wasn't enough space for expansion, and the school was moved to the northwest corner of 156th Street and Bennington Road in 1940. A new school was built that had a gymnasium and sports fields. Consolidation of rural schools into District 59 resulted in further expansion in 1957, 1964, and again in 1969. The district continues to experience rapid growth due to suburban expansion from Omaha.

The first known church service in the community was held in 1886 at the District 67 schoolhouse. The service resulted in the formation of the Zion Evangelical Lutheran congregation. One year later, the congregation had raised sufficient funds to procure land two miles south of town. It built a church that had two rooms: one for services and another for a Lutheran school.

Residents in Bennington founded St. John's Lutheran Church a decade later, in 1898. Pastor Ernst Walters accepted the calling. In less than a year, the congregation had built a new church and parsonage and had a loyal following. The church outgrew its facilities by 1925 and was enlarged and remodeled. Continued growth of both churches resulted in the construction of new facilities in the early 1960s.

The student body of Rural District 63 proudly poses in front of its one-room schoolhouse. Rural school districts were formed to meet the needs of their communities, and initially they were located within walking or riding distance of their students. Schools normally had one or two rooms and taught first through sixth grades. The little girl on the left in the polka-dot dress is Edna Mohr. When she started school, she could only speak German. After graduating sixth grade, she went on to earn a teaching certificate. She taught in several neighboring schools before teaching at Bennington, where she ended a distinguished 53-year career.

The Dornacker School was established in 1871 and was one of the first schools in the area. German settlers met at this school and decided to build the Dutch Hall, where they could practice their language and social customs. The Dornacker School was eventually consolidated into District 59.

George Mangold petitioned to have Bennington School District 59 created. The request identified only 680 acres, making it the smallest district in the state. Bennington's first school sat prominently on the highest hill in town on North Second Street between Molley and Stark Streets. It was built in 1892 and funded from $2,000 collected from liquor license fees from the town's four saloons.

The total student body of Bennington School District 59 is pictured in 1898. Today, the number of enrolled students has reached 2,500.

The Bennington School quickly ran out of space. Builders attempted to dig a basement in 1910 to provide much needed extra room. However, a severe rainstorm caused the ground to cave in, causing the building to collapse. The structure was totally ruined.

Bennington's second school was built in the same location as the first. The new school had two full stories and a basement. The school board had plans for the extra space.

The 1912 student body and two teachers proudly stand in front of Bennington Public School's new building. Only the first floor was finished before the first year of operations due to budget constraints. There was adequate funding the following year not only to finish construction but also to hire two additional teachers and add ninth and tenth grades.

Benson High School is pictured around 1913. Bennington initially only offered first through eighth grades at District 59. Ninth and tenth grades were added after 1912. Eleventh and twelfth grades were added after 1924. Prior to 1924, those wanting a high school education had to go to Benson, Omaha, or another neighboring high school.

The 1939 Badger quintet won the district basketball championship, beating Boy's Town in a low-scoring game of 19-9. From left to right are Gilbert White, John Mordhorst, coach Lynn Dankle, Robert Grant, Robert Dornacker, and David Richards.

The 1925 Bennington student body poses in front of the school. The young man sitting on a tricycle is Norman Mangold, one of the community's first victims of polio. The turn of the 20th century saw a polio epidemic that killed thousands. Norman contracted the disease as an infant and never fully recovered the use of his legs. He became an accomplished artist in spite of his handicap, and his portrait of his grandfather Peter Mangold hung in the Joslyn Art Museum. Small rural schools produced some very remarkable and gifted students.

Bennington Public School faculty is pictured in 1939. From left to right are Superintendent Lynn Dankle, Principal Maebelle Harris, Edna Mohr, Gretchen Goede, Wilma Witte, and Ruby Bohl.

It is believed this is a photograph of the 1919 Benson basketball team sporting an early school logo. Tenth grade was the highest offered by the Bennington School at that time. Bennington offered a high school education starting in 1924. (Courtesy of Nancy Neumeyer.)

Study hall at Bennington High School is pictured in 1951. From left to right are Ruth Gregerson, Deloris Gray Gottsch, Myra Kruse Nelson, and Elain Sass. (Courtesy LaMar Eicke.)

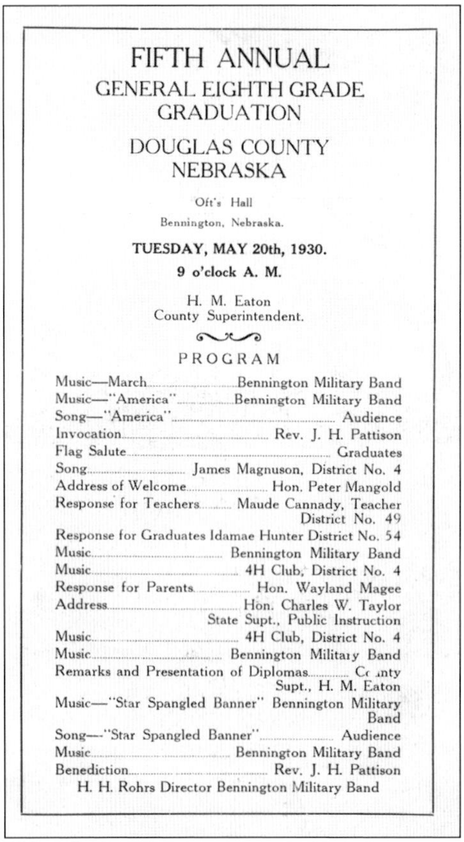

FIFTH ANNUAL
GENERAL EIGHTH GRADE
GRADUATION

DOUGLAS COUNTY
NEBRASKA

Oft's Hall
Bennington, Nebraska.

TUESDAY, MAY 20th, 1930.
9 o'clock A. M.

H. M. Eaton
County Superintendent.

PROGRAM

Music—March........Bennington Military Band
Music—"America"........Bennington Military Band
Song—"America"........Audience
Invocation........Rev. J. H. Pattison
Flag Salute........Graduates
Song........James Magnuson, District No. 4
Address of Welcome........Hon. Peter Mangold
Response for Teachers........Maude Cannady, Teacher District No. 49
Response for Graduates Idamae Hunter District No. 54
Music........Bennington Military Band
Music........4H Club, District No. 4
Response for Parents........Hon. Wayland Magee
Address........Hon. Charles W. Taylor State Supt., Public Instruction
Music........4H Club, District No. 4
Music........Bennington Military Band
Remarks and Presentation of Diplomas........County Supt., H. M. Eaton
Music—"Star Spangled Banner" Bennington Military Band
Song—"Star Spangled Banner"........Audience
Music........Bennington Military Band
Benediction........Rev. J. H. Pattison
H. H. Rohrs Director Bennington Military Band

The 1930 eighth-grade graduation ceremony was held at Oft's Hall in Bennington. The Bennington Juvenile Military Band provided the music. Douglas County rural schools started to consolidate eighth-grade graduation ceremonies in 1925.

The vast number of early schools were small and rural and graduated their students at a sixth- or eighth-grade level. A student commonly had to go elsewhere to attend high school. This diploma was issued by Douglas County and allowed students to attend a high school of their choice.

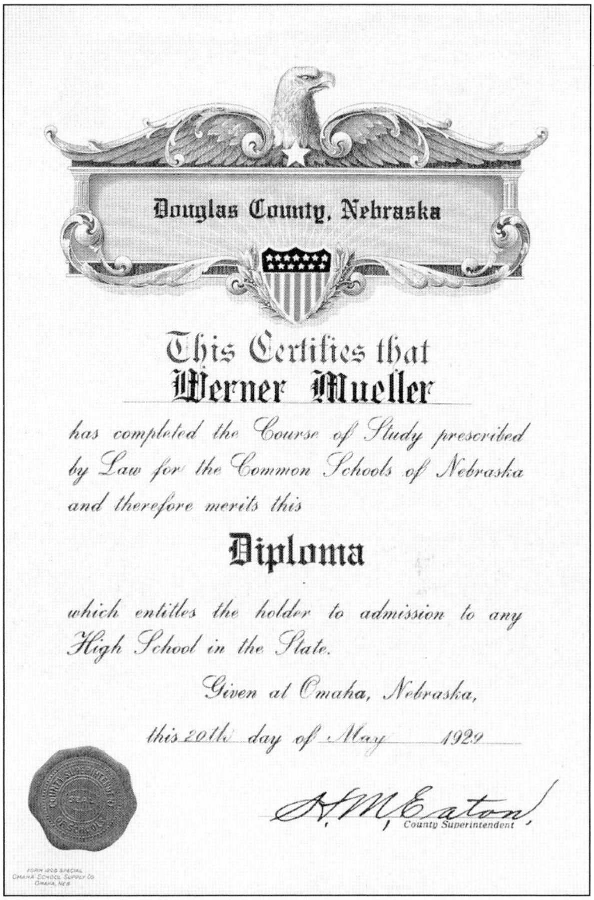

Douglas County, Nebraska

This Certifies that

Werner Mueller

has completed the Course of Study prescribed by Law for the Common Schools of Nebraska and therefore merits this

Diploma

which entitles the holder to admission to any High School in the State.

Given at Omaha, Nebraska,

this 20th day of May 1929

H. M. Eaton, County Superintendent

School zone, slow down! The rural schoolhouse in the background is District 62, which was about four miles southwest of Bennington around 1935. (Courtesy of Weyland Magee.)

This 1953 photograph shows the student body of Rural School District No. 40. The school was near 144th and Ida Streets in Omaha. From left to right are (first row) Dale Logemann, Melvin Logemann, Larry Buckles and Joe Kelly; (second row) Lois Brase, Carol Logemann, Marilyn Harder, Barbara Buckles, Phyllis Penke, and Margaret Ann Harder; (third row) Arthur Logeman, Suzanne Sorensen, Walter Harder Jr., Joan Markmann, and Sam Sorensen. Their teacher was Helen Mordhorst.

In 1948, Saint John's Lutheran Church held a golden anniversary celebration. Three previous pastors attended the celebration. From left to right are Rev. Robert Shirck (pastor from 1948 to 1957), Rev. Ernst Walter (1898–1900), Rev. Henry Goede (1932–1939), and Rev. Warren Churchill (1939–1947).

The Bennington Public School music class meets on the stage of the gymnasium around 1957. That year, the school was undergoing construction and in need of additional classroom space. The school was expanded to the north. More than half a dozen rooms, including administrative offices, home economics, and industrial art rooms, were added.

This is Bennington's class of 1941. It was the first class to graduate from the new school.

The student body of District 26 poses in front of its rural school, two miles west of Bennington. The teacher lived with the Adolf Mueller family on their farm half a mile away. Boarding with a local family was a common practice for rural teachers in 1915.

Schools were often crowded, and a classroom could be occupied by students of various ages. Early schools could be relatively dark, relying on old lamps for light. Electric lighting did not arrive in Bennington until nearly 1920.

It is believed that the first yearbook was produced by the students of District 59 in 1926 by the high school classes. It was dedicated to two teachers, Victor Bracke and Jeanette Kvam. It was reproduced using a typewriter, carbon paper, and original drawings. This is Clifford Petersen's artistic depiction of school life. (Courtesy of Lois Musel.)

The first church in the area was Zion Evangelical Lutheran Church, founded in 1886. A year later, a 24-foot-by-40-foot building was constructed two miles south of Bennington that served as both a church and a Lutheran school. A bell tower was added to the church in 1900, and a separate school was built at the same time. (Courtesy of Zion Evangelical Lutheran Church.)

Pastor Ernst Walters was asked to visit the Bennington community in 1898 to explore the possibility of starting a Lutheran church. He met with residents and held two services; the first attracted four people, the second 40. At the last sermon, the faithful decided to start St. John's Lutheran Church and elected Walters their pastor. He returned to Kansas with a promise of a $20 monthly salary and a place to live. He returned to Bennington with his wife and had to borrow funds to retrieve his household goods from the depot. Unfortunately, there was no home available, and the minister and his wife spent their first night in an upstairs room above the Storz Saloon. A beer delivery man helped them move their belongings in on a Saturday afternoon. That evening, it is said the saloon crowd serenaded the couple.

The community raised the necessary funds to build St. John's Lutheran Church and parsonage in four months. The church was constructed on the northeast corner of First and Molley Streets and finished in 1898.

The 1930 Confirmation class of St. John's poses on the front steps of the recently remodeled church. The congregation had outgrown its church, and in 1925, the building was enlarged and remodeled. Its orientation was changed from facing west to east.

The 1957 vacation Bible school students and teachers are assembled in front of Zion Evangelical Lutheran Church. Pastor Herbert Brase kneels at front right. (Courtesy of Dale Logemann.)

Pastor Lorin Wolff and others brave a cold January 12, 1962, to break ground for the new St. John's Lutheran Church. They watch as 91-year-old C.W. Glandt does the honors. Glandt had built the congregation's first church in 1898 and was the sole survivor of the church's original 13 charter members.

This photograph was taken in 1898, prior to the parsonage being built at St. John's Lutheran Church in Bennington.

St. John's Lutheran Church relocated and built a new church, which was dedicated in 1962 by Pastor Norman Schroeder. Two years later, Zion Evangelical Lutheran Church also built and dedicated a new church. Both churches were growing with the community.

Six

Community and Life

The ability to gather socially was important for early pioneer families. Early farm life on the prairie was lonely, especially for the women. Even the men appreciated the chance to get together and talk. Travel was slow and often difficult. Farm homes at that time were small due to the scarcity and expense of building materials; few of those early farmers even had barns. Their first community buildings were often rural schools and churches.

Many of the first farmers in this area came from northern Germany. A group of them met at the Dornacker School in 1875 to discuss the need for a social hall where they could meet and celebrate life with their friends. Forty-four farmers pledged $20 apiece and their labor to build a German or "Dutch" hall. Their families wanted a place where their community could celebrate. Money was borrowed, and work began the following year. Lumber was hauled in by horse and wagon from Omaha.

The hall was finished in 1876. It was bragged that the Dutch Hall had the best maple dancing floor west of the Missouri River. The hall also boasted a 33-foot bar, and it is reported that anyone who could see over the bar was served. The hall was the center of social and political life for decades.

Better and more easily accessible facilities became available as local communities grew. Nearly every small town had some sort of social hall where people could gather to listen to music, dance, and celebrate social events. Bennington had Oft's Hall and the Modern Woodmen of America Hall, Washington had a town hall, and Elkhorn had Denker's Hall.

Early farming and home making demanded a great deal of time and effort. Livestock had to be fed and taken care of morning and night. Farming with horses demanded long hours and strenuous work. Wives had children to take care of, and many sewed and mended their own cloths. They scrubbed clothes by hand, dried them on a clothesline, gardened, and canned much of their own food. Older children helped by pumping and carrying water for the kitchen, cleaning chamber pots, bringing in fuel and cleaning stoves, beating rugs to clean them, feeding the chickens, and gathering eggs.

Families are just as busy today, but machinery allows us to do our work much faster, providing more time for leisure activities. Just consider the time we spend on our phones, computers, televisions, participating in school sports and other curricular activities, and going out for dinner or to a movie.

This c. 1890s photograph shows a Schleswig-Holstein Verein gathering outside the Dutch Hall. Henry Schneider served as president, Rudolph Peters as secretary and manager, and Charles Gottsch as treasurer. The Dutch Hall provided a place where they could meet, support one another, and celebrate their native language, social customs, and life. Dances were held at least once a month and more often in good weather. They formed a chapter of the Plattdeutscher Verein, a fraternal

benefit society for those coming from lowland Germany. Membership was limited to 499. The organization helped members in need and offered a death benefit. When a member died, the surviving members would each pay a dollar to the deceased's family to help cover funeral costs. They also created the German Cemetery a short distance away.

The Dutch Hall is seen around 1960, at the end of its existence. Adolph Steffen had a farm just north of the Douglas-Washington County line, and he gave the Schleswig-Holstein Verein a 99-year lease to build its social hall on his land. The hall was torn down in the early 1960s, and the county line road was named Dutch Hall Road in memory of its importance. (Courtesy of the Washington County Museum.)

A combined gathering of the Royal Neighbors of America and Modern Woodmen of America is pictured here in Bennington around 1910. Both were fraternal benefit organizations started in the late 1880s and still in existence today. The Modern Woodmen were originally an all-male organization, while the Royal Neighbors were created by women.

A group has gathered in Bennington to celebrate the French defeat in the Franco-Prussian War of 1870, which marked the unification of Prussia. Schleswig and Holstein were two small separate nation states that became the northern provinces of Germany. While nationalism ran high with some Germans, many immigrated to America to avoid war.

The community responded to the nation's call to duty in World War I. Edward Gordon was mechanically inclined and became a chief mechanic in the Army's newly formed A Truck Company, 5th Division. Henry Ford sold the Army 10,000 Model T trucks to haul troops and supplies in Europe. Gordon served in France and returned to work for the Edison Company in Chicago. He returned to the Gordon farm during the Depression and lived there until his death.

Russell (left) and Lester Logemann are all dressed up with their white shirts and ties as they pose reluctantly next to the family's 1919 Ford Model T. They are probably heading to church and then to grandma's home for dinner. (Courtesy of Dale Logemann.)

Alexander and Lucy Gordon moved from Central City, Nebraska, to the Bennington area in 1910. They bought the prestigious Hollyrood Farm two miles west of Bennington. They purchased this amazing four-story Victorian home and 160 acres for $33,000. The house sat on a hill overlooking the valley and was said to have been built by a railroad executive.

Tornados are part of living in the Midwest. This is what was left of the Hollyrood home after the Easter Sunday storm of 1913. The storm ravaged eastern Nebraska, spawning eight tornados. The Gordon family saw the funnel cloud approach and found shelter in a nearby ravine as it tore their home apart. The storm's death toll reached over 170 people and remains the worst loss of human life from any storm in Nebraska's history.

Businessmen from Bennington and neighboring Florence meet at Oft's Hall for a banquet in 1939. Businesses were still recovering from the Depression, and networking helped people find new markets and better ways of doing business.

The burned-out remains of the Bennington House and Storz Saloon are seen following the 1913 fire. It was reported that a bar fight in Grothusen's Saloon started the fire. Strong winds spread the flames, setting half the business district on fire. Damaged or destroyed buildings included Oft's Hotel and Saloon, Paulsen's Saloon and opera house, Witte's drug store, Kirschner's garage, Otto Hansen's meat market, the Bennington House, the Storz Saloon, St. John's Lutheran Church, and three large barns.

T.E. Fletcher is moving a home up Allen Street around 1915. It took a well-disciplined team to work that close to a steam-powered tractor. Building materials were quite expensive, and lumber was reused whenever possible. Occasionally, a building would be partitioned into smaller sections for easier hauling, but sometimes an intact building was moved.

The Washington community often had potluck dinners in the upper floor of the Washington Hall, like this one pictured around 1950. Dances were initially held downstairs until the Knudsen family bought the building and set up their business downstairs. Dances were then moved upstairs with one rule: the Flying Dutchman was not allowed. This was a dance where participants would stomp in unison with enough force to cause structural damage. (Courtesy of LaMar Eicke.)

Farm sales were certainly not unusual, but during the late 1920s and 1930s, many were due to foreclosures triggered by delinquent mortgages or taxes. In some small communities, neighbors would often not bid against someone attempting to buy back their repossessed home or farm. The reason for this sale is unknown. (Courtesy of LaMar Eicke.)

Eggert and Rosa Oft celebrate their 25th anniversary with a party at their farm around 1907. Nearly 200 of their friends attended, and the couple was presented with an inscribed silver and crystal decanter. Eggert had reached the age of 60, and in three years, the couple would build a new home in Bennington.

Tim Ohrt served in the US Cavalry during World War I in Europe. He returned and married Ella Claussen in 1919 and settled in Bennington, where he started and ran a hardware store with Emil Stoltenberg for 30 years. A prominent community leader, he served on the village board for 24 years, 20 of them as chairman. He helped organize the Bennington Legion Post No. 266 and served as commander for 19 years. Ohrt also served as president of St. John's Church Council and the Bennington Volunteer Fire Department and served on the Bennington School Board. (Courtesy of Jodi Pooley.)

Here are some of the membership ribbons for the Bennington Plattdeutsch Verein, a society of people from northern Germany. The organization's goals were to perpetuate the Plattdeutsch dialect of the German language and its customs and to provide assistance and a death benefit to members.

Elvin Hoier's family settled just northwest of Bennington. He joined the US Navy in 1942, serving in the Atlantic convoys and in shipping along the East Coast of America. He was serving aboard a tanker carrying aviation gasoline when it was accidently rammed by another ship. The ocean was set ablaze, 88 died, and the ship sank. Hoier was one of only seven survivors. He suffered double pneumonia and pleurisy from his ordeal.

Bennington's first Girl Scout troop is pictured around 1958. St. John's Lutheran Church sponsored Girl and Boy Scout troops. From left to right are (first row) Kathie Peetz, Carol Biesendorfer, Ann Rushton, and Brenda Hatfield; (second row) Twila Logemann, Alice Rushton, Carole Sorensen, Elizabeth Wolff, and Sandra Petersen; (third row) Diane Muller, Alice Rushton (leader), Jean Laaker, Pastor Loren Wolff, Judy Kruse, Barbra Rawlings, Jean Biesendorfer (assistant leader), and Nancy Villwok.

Boiler mate Dale Mohr is seen in the engine room of the destroyer USS *Bausell* (DD-845). Mohr graduated from Bennington High School in 1949 and served four years in the Navy during the Korean War. He married Ila Kruse, ran the Bennington Hardware Store, and then built the Bennington Gamble Store. He served on the church council, town board, and Bennington Volunteer Fire Department, and was a member of the American Legion and VFW. (Courtesy of Susan Mohr.)

Uniforms were fashionable during World War II, even with children's apparel. LeMara Misfeldt (left) and Marybeth Knudson have on their uniforms while patrolling on their bicycles and practicing their salutes around 1944. (Courtesy of LaMar Eicke.)

When the country went to war, it needed money. Savings bond drives came to every corner of America, including Bennington. Here, Harold Roe, president of the Bank of Bennington, poses with an assistant in front of a Series E savings bond. The government issued Series E bonds during World War II. Harold's father, C.F. Roe, purchased the bank in 1928, and it remains the oldest family-owned business in Bennington.

War broke out and men were being called into service. Couples who were contemplating marriage had a decision to make—whether to wait or get married. Paul and Jerry Pooley got married at St. John's Lutheran Church before he was deployed. He returned from the war, and the couple became prominent members of the community.

Jeanette and Enno Mueller are receiving their wedding guests at Oft's Hall. Communities celebrated weddings, anniversaries, and other social events. Wedding and anniversary dances were commonly open to the general public, since many in the small community knew each other and were interrelated. Couples who married in the 1930s, 1940s, and 1950s generally met their future spouse at one of these gatherings.

Bennington Public School's first aid class is pictured in 1945. World War II triggered a keen interest in community preparedness, and knowing first aid was important regardless of age.

The community had been collecting donations to purchase a fire truck for years. That dream came true in 1947, when it bought a Ford pumper truck. On its arrival, volunteers drove up and down the city's streets honking its horn to the cheers of the residents. Prior to that, residents were totally dependent upon neighboring towns like Irvington and Elkhorn for fire fighting.

St. John's Lutheran Church sponsored Boy and Girl Scout troops. Here, Bennington's first Cub Scout troop is meeting in the church's basement in 1952.

Family and friends held a send-off party for Thomas Backhuus (third from left), who was entering the Army during World War II. The party was at Peony Park in Omaha. (Courtesy of Nancy Mohr.)

A parade was held on June 15, 1952, to honor Dr. C.W. Hickey for his 50-plus years of service to the community. Bennington also celebrated with a baseball game and, of course, a dance. This float was created by the Missionary Society and depicted the Hickeys' wedding in 1907. Mangold's Red & White store is seen in the background.

This photograph was taken about 1915 showing the arrival of the Fremont Boosters in Bennington. Car tours were becoming popular. In the background are, from left to right, Kirschner's store and post office, Mangold and Glandt's Bank, and the Modern Woodmen of America hall. Diedrich Kirschner moved his entire building two lots to the east and sold the corner lots to Peter Mangold and C.W. Glandt for their new bank in 1914.

Seven

Recreation and Free Time

There were various forms of entertainment on the frontier. The most popular were church functions, potluck dinners, and dances. Nearly all those in the Bennington area who married in the 1930s, 1940s, and 1950s met their spouses at a public dance. The first dances were held at the Dutch Hall, but with time, dance or social halls began showing up in all the new communities. Public dances were commonly held monthly, and during good weather, they were held more frequently. Wedding and anniversary dances were commonly opened up to the entire community.

Communities also supported annual festivals and fairs, a practice that continues today. Bennington's Harvest Festival started in 1908 and has transitioned to Bennington Daze, which is now celebrated in June. Town baseball clubs were another important pastime, but that emphasis has switched toward youth sport clubs and high school and American Legion baseball.

Frontier families had far less free time. Children had farm chores to do, including helping with crops and livestock and helping mother with the garden, laundry, canning, and housework. However, when they did get some free time, they enjoyed playing games and baseball, fishing, shooting, hunting, swimming, horse racing, and livestock and farming competitions. A popular place to play was Papio Creek. All it took was a little imagination and free time to find something interesting to do.

A Fourth of July parade makes its way down Stark Street toward the depot and Bennington Park. Folks are all dressed up and lining the street for the celebration. There is little doubt of what followed: a baseball game, food and drink, and an evening dance.

From left to right, William, Arthur, and Raymond Lage lived on a farm north of Bennington where their parents settled in 1878. Here the boys are playing with an old wheelbarrow, a sawhorse, and their pets, two dogs and a turkey. A healthy imagination helped children of rural families find things to do. It helped if there were wheels. That is how the soapbox derby got started in Dayton, Ohio, in 1934: imagination, wheels, old boxes, and some free time.

Charles William (C.W.) Hadan came to Bennington as a young man in 1915. He is shown here with friends in a boat they probably built on Papio Creek, just downstream from the 156th Street bridge. Hadan bought a plumbing shop in 1918 and later opened up a new store on South Second Street called C.W. Hadan Plumbing-Heating-Electric. One of his favorite pastimes was to take a group of town kids fishing. He was the first recipient of Bennington's Outstanding Citizen Award.

Members of the Bennington Rifle Club pose with their rifles and membership ribbons around 1889. Their rifles were all single-shot bench rifles. Marksmanship was a cherished skill and recreational pastime. (Courtesy of Loren Cohrs.)

Charles Fredrick Gottsch was an expert marksman who won the national rifle championship in 1886. Marksmanship was an important pioneer skill. Someone handy with a rifle was more apt to bring home fresh meat, protect livestock from predators, and protect the family. Shooting was a popular sport that endured in the community for many years, especially with the rural residents. (Courtesy of Brent Gottsch.)

From left to right, Ben Petersen, Henry Neumeyer, and Edward Paulsen have borrowed Bert Seymour's car for a test drive around 1915. They are driving on 156th Street in front of the Oft-Gordon House. Man's love of the wheel was enhanced with its connection to the motor.

The Bennington Juvenile Military Band is pictured around 1925. The band gave concerts at Oft's Hall and other venues and won several music competitions during its 11-year existence from 1923 to 1934. The band was directed by H.H. Rohr and managed by Otto Gottsch.

Hunting was a popular pastime that also brought meat to the kitchen table. Nearly every farm boy had a .22 rifle, and squirrels and rabbits were popular game. This young man is showing off a bag of 11 fox squirrels as he poses behind his 1917 Harley Davidson motorcycle.

Town baseball was the recreational mainstay of America; nearly every town had its hometown team. Rivalry between neighboring towns could be intense. The 1922 Bennington team had an excellent record due to pitcher Robert Harris (first row, third from left). In actuality, Harris was a ringer. He lived in Omaha and was paid to pitch. Go Bennington!

Annual events at Bennington Park drew hundreds of visitors. The park became a popular place to hold parties and social events. The city held its first annual Harvest Festival there in 1908. The festivities included a parade, a baseball game, athletic competitions, horse racing, judging of farm and home produce, and an evening dance. The railroad often scheduled a night special to take folks home after the festivities.

Seven young ladies from Bennington show off their 1915 swimsuit fashions. Valley and Arlington were neighboring towns that had lakes with swimming beaches. What could be more delightful than a 15-mile drive through the countryside to enjoy a cool swim, some healthy sunbathing, and a picnic, while possibly meeting some new boys?

From left to right, Roy, Jeanette, and Nancy Gordon are boating at Valley, Nebraska, around 1926. Valley had a lake by the Platte River that offered swimming and a boat rental.

This empty field conveniently served as a ballfield and park until the Bennington Volunteer Fire Department built a fire station here. Beyond the players is the two-story Koch Hotel, and to the far right is Bunz's Implement Dealership.

A party of Bennington girls enjoys swimming at the Valley lakes in 1910. Kids would often go to Arlington or Valley for swimming parties. The gristmill pond and creek offered swimming, but it was reported that swimmers entering those waters had a better than even chance of exiting with a leech or two.

These were the first planes to land near Bennington; they arrived in August 1920. Barnstorming and interest in flying peaked as aviators returned from World War I. Pilots would advertise and schedule appearances in towns across the country to exhibit their daredevil flying skills and offer rides. Air shows were as popular then as they are today.

Folks are gathering at Bennington Park for an evening dance. The park grounds were owned by the Bunz family, and the acreage had several buildings. The one seen here had several uses. This evening, it is serving as a dance pavilion, but during the week, one might see boys playing basketball here, and in late fall and winter, it held baled hay and equipment.

Bennington's Harvest Festival Parade participants are gathered south of the railroad depot. It appears that they might be awaiting the arrival of a train.

The Nebraska Parks Commission introduced ring-neck pheasants in 1911; it released 500 birds throughout the state. Twenty years later, pheasant hunting had become a popular outdoor sport. Pheasant under glass was no longer limited to the affluent. This hunt occurred in 1934 on the Harold Roe farm.

Enno Mueller and his sister Doris sit on his new 1946 Indian motorcycle at their parents' farm west of Bennington. Enno ordered the motorcycle during World War II, but manufacturing had been diverted toward the war effort. His order finally arrived in 1946, after hostilities had ended.

Here a family is out for a sleigh ride. After a few inches of snow, a sleigh was an effective mode of travel. Winter travel was cold, and in addition to warm clothing, riders often carried lap blankets that were generally a quilt-lined cow or horse hide. They were water- and windproof and quite warm.

Peetz Place was a popular hangout for people of all ages. Arthur and Elsia Peetz managed a café, pool hall, and bar. These high school students are hanging out in front of the building in 1955. The establishment offered nickel soft drinks, generous servings of ice cream, and 25¢ hamburgers. Arthur Peetz also served in the Bennington Volunteer Fire Department; during a 1958 call, he suffered a heart attack that forced him to retire.

Dances were extremely popular social events. Nearly every town, regardless of size, had a dance hall or a room large enough for dancing. The Storz Saloon had a large room upstairs that was used for parties and small social events. This photograph shows a square dance club using that space in 1939.

These three darling children have gotten their homemade clothing a little dirty while playing. During the Depression, feed and flour companies used patterned sacking material that could be repurposed to make hand towels and children's clothing.

The automobile offered couples a wide range of recreational opportunities they simply did not have with a horse and buggy. Cars provided easier travel, and they were more dependable, faster, and more romantic. A new car made an impression, as it does today!